Make New Year Resolutions
– AND KEEP THEM
USING NLP!

Donna Blinston

Paperback ISBN13 9781904312840

Kindle/Mobipocket ISBN 9781907685200

ePub/iBooks ISBN 9781907685194

Published in the UK by MX Publishing, 335, Princess Park Manor,

Royal Drive, London, N11 3GX www.mxpublishing.co.uk

Cover Design by www.staunch.com

Authorised Publishers and Distributor for SAARC countries

ANLP (India) Press

Donna Blinston is a certified trainer of Neuro Linguistic Programming (NLP) and the founder of Inspirational Solutions in your hands consultancy, trained by the only recognised trainers of NLP accredited by Kingston University. Inspirational Solutions started out as a one to one life coaching consultancy service, as the business has progressed additional partners with Business, HR and ICT backgrounds have been enlisted to develop Inspirational Solutions into the bespoke training and consultancy organisation it is today.

"I have always been passionate about developing myself and others. I love learning and feel privileged to be a part of helping others to learn and develop. I first found out about NLP in January 2005 when I attended a NLP Diploma course down in Cardiff. This changed my life in so many ways. I discovered what is important to me and more importantly, focused on what I wanted out of life. I was able to appreciate other people's point of view and build better personal and professional relationships. My professional life developed profoundly, which only increased my passion for finding out more about NLP".

By background, Donna Blinston is a professional staff nurse in an ICU-Intensive Care Unit and intends to bring NLP techniques into common practice in the NHS. After dealing with a range of clients she has realised that the realms of NLP are limitless, with different techniques and practices lending themselves to benefit professionals from other professional backgrounds. Each course has been specifically designed for their target audience and will enable professionals to reach their full potential, get what they want out of their career and enjoy their work.

Contents

Chapter 1: Introduction

> *"Whether you think you can or you think you can't,*
> *you're probably right"*
> Henry Ford

"This year, I will go to the gym",

***"This** year, I will stop eating chocolate ",*

***"THIS** year, I will lose weight".*

Do any of these New Year's resolutions sound familiar? More than likely, most of us have created New Year's resolutions similar to these. But how many of us have actually STUCK to our resolutions?

The purpose of this book is to show the reader the benefits of Neuro linguistic programming (NLP) in a goal setting tense.

It has been written for readers who have heard of NLP but are not interested in studying the whole diploma before they see the practical real life benefits it has to offer. *Make New Year resolutions-AND KEEP THEM USING NLP!* is an extract from *Psychobabble: A strait forward, plain English guide to the Benefits of NLP*, showing chapters 5: Goals and well formed Outcomes and Chapter 8: Submodalities, that is the importance of making well formed outcomes and then actually visualising that they have achieved them in the present day, seeing the benefits of the goal in its entirety, making it more "realistic" and desirable to boost motivation to achieve it. The additional benefit of this is to highlight any incongruence's in you and the goal that would arise preventing you from achieving it.

Author's previous works;

Psychobabble: A strait forward, plain English guide to the Benefits of NLP, is a practical textbook written in plain English enabling you to navigate the jargon of Neuro Linguistic programming and realise the practical techniques this new science can bring you.

After introducing what NLP is and how it originated, the NLP Diploma is then broken down into techniques organised by chapter. Each chapter then follows the same layout, further broken down giving a real world definition, the benefits, the history and /or science, a reference structure and real life examples of using the technique. With the chapter finishing with examples of when and how to use the technique and practical exercises for the reader to learn and develop the technique further for themselves.

More importantly this textbook shows the practical benefits NLP can bring to a wide audience, making it ideal for recommended reading for students studying this subject or supplementary reading for most Business & Management Degrees, Healthcare courses or simply for professionals in management and leadership positions.

Make New Year resolutions - AND KEEP THEM USING NLP!

What is a New Year resolution? Why do we make them? To me a New Year resolution is a Goal I wish to make, motivated by the coming of a New Year and the ending of the old. Almost giving me permission to let go of the past and motivate me to look towards the future.

This is what makes New Year resolutions fantastic; they fall down because they are often made on the spur of the moment or in a drunken embrace with a friend! Surely the coming of a New Year and the end of an old requires more respect than this? By understanding, respecting and treating a New Year resolution as a goal we start on our first step towards achieving them.

This extract focuses on goal setting and achievement through the well formed outcomes technique. This is the term used in NLP to describe a process of systematically refining goals, objectives or targets so that they fulfil the criteria. The process is similar but is more thorough than that of the more widely-known S.M.A.R.T goals technique. When our wants, dreams or wishes are refined using this process they become more believable and realistic, which is why they are then described as being 'well-formed' outcomes

> _The world makes way for the man who knows where he is going._
> Ralph Waldo Emerson

The NLP goes beyond the concept of goal setting by using desired outcome development. 'Goal' is a general term and does not specify the actions to be taken in order to generate the desired outcome, whereas an outcome is highly specific. An outcome signifies a specific goal development strategy, providing a better understanding of the steps to be taken. Well formed outcomes can be applied on a personal, professional or organisational basis. This abstract looks into what makes goals successful, whilst highlighting potential reasons why goals have not been met previously.

How? Well once you have designed your well formed outcome, you will be introduced to submodalities, which are how we code, order and give meaning to our experiences, therefore having a great impact upon how we perceive what goes on around us. We are only able to hold a limited amount of information in our minds at any one time. The well-formed outcome model will help you to create highly detailed images, sounds, feelings and words (internal representation) related to the outcome. These internal representations will enhance your abilities, resources and skills for achieving the outcome. By using submodalities and changing these finer details we can change our attitudes towards our goals and further empower ourselves towards achieving it.

"One ship sails East,
And another West,
By the self-same winds that blow,
Tis the set of the sails
And not the gales,
That tells the way we go".

Ella Wheeler Wilcox

Chapter 2: - NL What?!

There are many definitions of NLP, from the illustrious and vague: "*How we use the language of the mind to consistently achieve our specific and desired outcomes*" (Richard Bandler)

> *It isn't where you come from, it's where you're going that counts.* Ella Fitzgerald

to the more plain English and assessable: "*A model of interpersonal communication chiefly concerned with the relationship between successful patterns of behaviour and the subjective experiences (esp. patterns of thought) underlying them*" and "*a system of alternative therapy based on this which seeks to educate people in self-awareness and effective communication, and to change their patterns of mental and emotional behaviour*" (Oxford English Dictionary).

We shall start with Richard Bandler, the Godfather of NLP if you like:

Richard Bandler (thankfully!) also describes NLP as "*An attitude and methodology that leaves behind a trail of techniques*". Explaining that an attitude of wanton curiosity and a willingness to experiment to understand how things work, leaves behind (gives the user) an increased range of skills and techniques that benefit their daily life. This hunger to understand how things work leads to discovering and taking on the beliefs, values and behaviours found in people who are outstanding in their respective fields, to utilise and benefit yourself and others.

Sue Knight (2002) reinforces this statement in her definition that NLP is "*The study of what works in thinking, language and behaviour. It is a way of coding and reproducing excellence that enables you to consistently achieve the results that you want both for yourself, for your business and for your life*"

To me, NLP is simply an established set of principles for teaching, learning and personal development that provide you with a variety of strategies for maximising both your professional performance and business /career potential.

So why the Silly name?

Let's break Neuro Linguistic programming down; Neuro, is understanding the patterns in our thinking. By understanding we can learn how these patterns influence the results we are getting in our work and personal life. Therefore the key to finding personal and business success comes primarily from within ourselves and learning about how we think enables us to utilise our inner resources.

Linguistic; is appreciating that what we say is what we think we can (and can't) do. Learning to understand and master the structure of our language is essential in a world where we increasingly trade through our ability to communicate.

> *"Argue for your limitations, and sure enough they're yours"* Richard Bach

Finally, Programming; we run our lives by having strategies /goals /objectives, very similar to how a computer uses a program to achieve a specific result. By realising and understanding the strategies we use to run our lives we give ourselves greater choice: choice to do more of the same or choice to enhance our potential and our individual excellence.

In essence, NLP is the study of our thinking, behaviour and language patterns so that we can build sets of successful strategies that work for us in making decisions. NLP can be described as the study of the mind and body link and the direct effect they have on each other. If you believe that you can achieve something then your positive state will enable you to find the resources to achieve it.

We will now look at the founding principles that apply to the contents of this book:

7

NLP Communication Model

To understand how we take information into our neurology and how that affects our behaviour, there is the NLP "model of communication". It is based on the notion that our five senses; sight, hearing, touch, taste and smell, take in two million bits of information at any one moment. Our conscious mind however, is only able take in approximately 126 bits of information during this same time period.

In order to compensate for this vast difference the mind filters the events our senses take in by deleting, distorting and generalising the information through our language, memories, attitudes, values, beliefs, decisions, etc. We then make an internal representation of the world we are taking in, with pictures, sounds and feeling. That puts us in a state of mind, which can change our physiology that affects our behaviour. All this happens in a fraction of a second and none of it has to happen in any particular order. We are in a constant state of flux, where our physiology can affect our attitudes towards achieving a goal just as easily as our behaviour can affect our language.

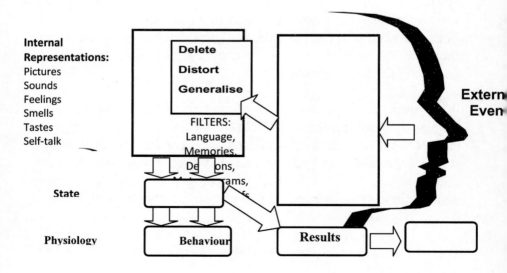

The communication model shows how we as humans interpret the world differently. Carolyn Boyes (2006) explains that we are all unique individuals that have our own set of rules, which govern how we interact with people, how we talk to ourselves and how we choose what we focus on and achieve. At any one time during your waking experience, you are being bombarded by over 2 million bits of sensory (light, sound, feeling, tastes and smells) information. We unconsciously filter out the information which is irrelevant to our cause. We leave out the unnecessary so that we can reduce the incoming information to what matters to us at that time.

Boyes (2006) goes on to state that these filters do the job of deleting, distorting and generalising according to our model of the world. Each second these 2 million bits of information come in through our senses and are filtered through our memories, beliefs and values, decisions, meta-programs (how you react to information given to you due to your personality traits i.e. how you conceptualise, perceive and comprehend information, or in short; what we do and don't pay attention to) and your idea of time /space, matter and energy. At the end of this process you're left with your perception. This perception is your internal representation (representation) of the external information around you when it is reduced down from 2 million bits to 126 bits. All internal representations are made up of images, sounds and sensations that constitute our model or image (belief) of the world. These are instantly translated through the nervous system (neurology) and expressed as chemicals in the body (emotion) which then influence our actions (behaviour). Because of this process how we perceive reality can be completely different to the person stood next to us, who generalises this information down to another set of 126 bits of

> *"What we see and hear is what we think about. What we think about is what we feel. What we feel influences our reactions. Reactions become habits and it is our habits that determine our destiny."* Bob Gass

9

information and experience their own version of reality, therefore reality is not "out there" but how we filter it to be.

Knowing this we can start to appreciate that basically what you believe is your result – The same event can, depending on your beliefs and values, give different internal representations. We delete portions of experience determined by our ability to handle abstract data and a preference for absorbing data into more manageable chunks, we then further generalise the event on past learned experiences and behavioural responses and finally distort the event by interpreting it in a way that best fits our internal world.

Deleting, Distorting and Generalising explained.

Delete - This is when we omit data or selectively pay attention to certain experiences and not to others. Think of a time when you were so engaged in a conversion that you were unaware of the other events going on around you, i.e. in a restaurant. Have you walked down the street with a friend of the opposite sex and later that day when you are back at home they ask you your views on the new phone /game /computer /electrical shop, which you didn't even see! You then talk about the girl with the bright green hair, or new clothes /handbag shop which they didn't notice.

A further example of this would be right now; as you are reading this book you won't have been aware of the feeling of your back in the chair or of the feeling of the socks on your feet until I mentioned it.

Distort – Distortions are when we misrepresent our reality. A distortion is the alteration of the original shape of an object, image, sound, or other form of information or representation. This is when you distort reality, i.e. can you imagine this room in red? Another example of distorting reality is when you and another person both go to see the same film or to the same meeting but you both have a different interpretation of what you saw /heard.

10

Generalise – Stereotyping generalisations are ideas or conclusions that have a general application /thing in common. It is putting ideas, people or things into a convenient group or category, or drawing global conclusions. This is why you don't have to re-learn how to drink from a different glass as you have generalised that it would be the same as drinking from any other glass you have used.

Watch out for the filters you place in your world, for the world is never what we think it to be. If we are taking in 2 million bits of information and only aware of around 126 bits, there is much data we are missing. The words we use are not actually the event or the item they represent; although they describe the event we have chosen them to represent the words themselves are not the actual event itself. We create our own reality based on our past experience. Our language becomes a 'map' of the 'territory' of our constructed reality, through the information we have obtained through our five senses. We code, order and give meaning (through deletion, distortion and generalisation) to our experience in words, sounds, pictures, feelings, tastes and smells. Five different people might all experience the same event but each will take a different experience away from it depending on their own beliefs and values.

Therefore in goal setting terms how we think of the goal and more importantly how we state the goal when setting it is vitally important to whether we can achieve it.

Presuppositions of NLP – Convenient assumptions

These are the founding principles of NLP, which when utilised, will provide you with a framework for learning and understanding the techniques in the following chapters. Some of these principles are going to be alien to you, try not to dismiss them out of hand; we have all lived a good life by our own principles, so what harm will come of trying new ones? An unfortunate example of this is after 10 years of playing squash an old man tapped on the gallery window and told me I was holding my racket wrong. Rubbish I thought, my serves are powerful and returns are low. The old man kindly (rudely!) took my racket and explained where my thumb and forefingers were meant to be placed and then went on to say I had the hardest job of all, as I had been playing for so long I had to put my old technique aside and will have to adopt this new technique. I will be truthful and say at first it was not easy, and sometimes I slipped into my old habits. But by staying firm and practicing, I am happy to say I have become a better squash player. The bad news I'm afraid is that this applies to you adopting these principles below;

A. **Respect for the other persons "Model of the World".** In order to create change effectively in another person, you do not have to believe what they believe, but simply respect and seek to understand it, and then you can seek to be understood. Talking in a way and using examples that appeals to their values and beliefs. Think back to the communication model; we all see the world differently because we all delete, distort and generalise differently dependant on our background and personal makeup. The other person's model of the world is right for them.

B. **The meaning and outcome of communication is in the response you get.** Again all about taking responsibility for your results. We are taught by communicating our thoughts and feelings clearly that the other person should understand our meaning. In truth; that other person will only respond to what they think you have said. You can only determine how effectively you are communicating by the response you get. By taking responsibility for your communication you can stress the importance of what you are saying, gauging on the other persons response as to whether they have actually completely understood it. If you do not receive the response you were expecting then what is it about your communication that they have not understood.

C. **The mind and the body affect each other.** Very *"Matrix-esk"*?! The mind and the body are one interconnected unit and so it is not possible to make changes in one without the other being affected. If you believe you can or you believe you can't you are most probably right. When you set about a task with a negative mindset that you cannot do it then you will struggle and /or fail. Changing your mindset will increase your opportunities for success. One example of the mind-body link is the feel good factor after exercise.

D. **The map is not the territory.** The words we use are not actually the event or the item they represent. Although they describe the event we have chosen them to represent the words themselves are not the actual event itself. We create our own reality based on our past experience. Our language becomes a 'map' of the 'territory' of our constructed reality, through the information we have obtained through our five senses. We code, order and give meaning (through deletion, distortion and generalisation) to our experience in words, sounds, pictures, feelings, tastes and smells. Five different people might all experience the same event but each will take a different experience away from it depending on their own beliefs and values. NLP is the art of changing our map to create more choices.

E. People are doing the best they can with the resources they have available. A person's behaviour is adaptable to the situation, their present behaviour is simply the best choice available to them with the resources they have available at that time, and their behaviour has a positive intention for them. Their behaviour is not who they are; by accepting the person you can support and assist them to change their behaviour into a more positive resourceful state.

Just as "Bob" who is given 5 minutes to prepare a presentation. Bob's presentation will be the best he can deliver with the resources he has available to him, drawing on his current level of knowledge and the examples /experience that he has had. Another person, "Tom" who is more experienced than Bob may give a better presentation. Just as Bob would if he had been given more notice and time to; prepare, research more data, and acquire and use props.

F. Behaviour is geared towards adaption. A person's behaviour is their response towards a situation; it is their level of understanding. Presenting the behaviour of confusion is done to find and gain understanding. Their behaviour is not the person themselves, it is simply just the way the person can represent their feelings /understanding. By knowing that their behaviour is due to a lack of understanding enables you to support that person by giving them the additional information that they need to change. This links back to the NLP presupposition: people are doing the best with the resources they have available. When realised people can change their behaviour and make it more appropriate to who they have become or who they wish to be, their behaviour is adaptable as new resources are available.

G. Pay attention to behaviour. Actions speak louder than words, behaviour is the truest and best quality information people can give to you. Notice the incongruence's between what a person says and what their body language says, and get

> *"Nothing is more revealing than behaviour"*
> Martha Graham

curious, ask questions like: *"Are you sure that this is ok?" "Do you want me to go over that again?" "Do you understand?"* Remember we all delete, distort and generalise differently through our own unique set of filters. So maybe you were explaining it in a way that prevented it going through. Once you start to see congruence you will know that they have understood.

H. Behaviour and change are to be evaluated in terms of context and ecology. All meaning is context dependant, however most of what is said is taken out of context and so it is important for information to be placed back into its original context to understand its true meaning. Behaviour is created specifically to the context and the reality currently being experienced, whether this behaviour is good, bad, useful or useless, it was adapted to the situation in which it was created. When doing change work with another, ensure it is ecological to that person. Because if it is not, then not only are you going to struggle, but these changes will be short lived and the negative consequences will outweigh the positive intention. Evaluate behaviour and change in terms of what the person is capable of becoming, and the impact it will have on the person's life overall.

I. People have all the resources they need to make the changes they want. People themselves are not un-resourceful, they are simply experiencing un-resourceful states, which when changed allows them to access all the resources within them to accomplish whatever they choose.

J. Possible in the world and possible for me is only a matter of how. There are no limitations in a person's ability to learn. If another person in broadly similar circumstances to me is capable of performing a behaviour /task, then it is possible for me too, or at least improve my own performance through learning.

K. The system (person) with the most flexibility (choices) of behaviour will have the most influence on the system. For those of you who study NLP, you will recognise this as the law of requisite variety. Basically the more options you have available to you the greater the chance of change and success.

L. There is no failure, only feedback. If a person does not succeed in something, this does not mean they have failed, it just means they have not succeeded yet. It took Erickson over 700 attempts to create the light bulb, and like him we can all vary our behaviour and be more positive to find a different way to achieve our

> *"I have learnt more from my failures than my successes"*
> Richard Branson

outcome. We can all learn from our mistakes, by having this mindset we are able to pick ourselves up and get on with it. Simply put: If what you are doing is not getting the results you want, try something different.

M. There are no resistant clients, only inflexible communicators. This resistance is a sign of a lack of rapport and can be broken down by being more flexible with your communication to appeal to the client's beliefs and values to create a climate of trust and co-operation. Think to yourself, how can I explain this differently in order for the other person to understand what I have said?

N. All procedures should increase choice and develop greater personal flexibility. Your goal being to increase the choices you have available to you now, opening more doors, giving you more options for your future /the situation you are in. For example; going on a particular course could enable you to develop professionally. Your learning will be increased if this course opens more doors for you both personally and professionally by increasing your flexibility; a goal beyond a goal.

O. All procedures should increase wholeness. Fewer parts mean more congruence and less conflict.

P. Change can be quick easy and lasting as long as you are clear on what and why you want to make the change, ensuring that it is ecological for you and those around you.

Q. We are in charge of our mind and therefore our results. If we are not getting the results we want then it is up to us to change the way we are going about it until we get the results we want. If we do not achieve something then it's only ever our fault and our responsibility to change in order to achieve what we want as other people will not change for you.

Now that you have understood the communication model and the presuppositions of NLP, I wish to introduce the concept of Ecology, which is simply checking that the goal you wish to make is congruent with your values and believes and the resources you have available.

Ecology - Does what you are planning comply with your values?

One day, a wealthy businessman hired a fishing boat to take him out to sea for a day of relaxation. The sun was shining, and the wealthy man took a liking to the happy young fisherman who guided the fishing boat through the waters of the harbour.

"Young man" called the wealthy businessman. *"I can teach you the secrets of success, if you would only listen carefully".*

"Ok" said the young fisherman, smiling as he cleaned the mornings catch.

Although he was a bit taken back by the young man's casual manner, the businessman began his lesson.

"First off, double your prices. You run a good clean boat and you know where the fish are plentiful".

"Why would I do that?" replied the young fisherman, distracted by a small crab playing in the waves by the shore.

The businessman could feel the irritation rising as he replied; *"because then you will be able to buy a second boat, then a third, and you will be able to take more tourists and catch more fish. If you work hard, you will earn enough to buy a whole fleet of boats".*

"But why would I want to do that?" the young fisherman asked as he rolled over onto his back to soak up the last gentle rays of the afternoon sun.

By now the wealthy businessman was becoming furious.

"Because then you will become rich, and you can hire people to do your work for you while you spend your days fishing and relaxing in the sun!"

"Ah" said the young fisherman, nodding sagely. *"That sounds wonderful!"*

In NLP, ecology deals with the relationships between you and your natural, social and created environments and how a proposed goal or change might affect on your relationships and environment. It is a frame within which the desired outcome is checked against the potential consequences in your life. It treats your relationship with self as a system and your relationship with others as subsystems that all interact.

Therefore when someone considers a change it is important to take into account the consequences of this change on the system as a whole. One of the main goals and intentions of NLP is to help people choose goals and make changes that achieve a sense of personal congruency and integrity with all other aspects of their life. If a change is proposed that is not ecological it will either not work, only be short lived, or the negative consequences will outweigh the positive intention of the change, therefore producing a negative result.

Ecology is the study of consequences and the impact of your action on the wider system. When you are setting an outcome you will want to consider what effect that outcome will have, not only on yourself, but on other people and the environment in which you operate. For example, if you change the way you work, that change may have an impact on your manager, your team, your customers, your suppliers and /or your family. Whether you are setting outcomes for yourself, or helping someone else set one, carrying out an ecology check enables you to set outcomes that will fit all aspects of your /their life.

In setting outcomes, we need to consider the consequences of achieving that outcome very carefully. Ecology is having an awareness of the overall system and an Ecology Check is tracking the consequences of the change made in all aspects of that system. An ecology check on any outcome, assists us to recognise the impact of that change in all systems of which we are a part, ranging from people very close to us, quickly zooming out to the society you are apart, the county you reside in to the planet generally!

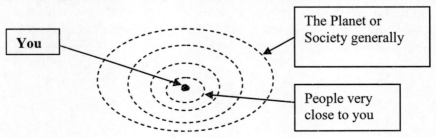

19

Ecology is a huge topic which is further expanded upon in NLP Practitioner and Master Practitioner levels. It is fair to say Ecology simply cannot be covered in a summary foundation chapter. However in the context of this book I am simply using Ecology to make you aware of how important it is to consider how the plans or any change you make will impact on you, your family, career, time available, money, etc. This book simply wishes to make you aware of whether the outcome of which you are planning conflicts with your beliefs and values.

Because if the outcome does conflict with your values and beliefs, then no matter how strenuously and articulacy you plan, you shall never achieve your true outcome.

Ecological self check questions;

- For what purpose do you want this?
- What will you gain or lose if you have it?
- What will happen if you get it?
- What won't happen if you get it?
- What will happen if you don't get it?
- What won't happen if you don't get it?

Most importantly: Are there any negative consequences in achieving this goal?

By looking at all options /questions /goals and opportunities in this way allows you to increase your own personal success, ensuring you are clear about what you want and what you want is clear. It is an awful situation to be in a year down the line when you realise that this goal /target /decision is not right for you, aren't you better finding this out at the beginning?

Chapter 3

Goals & Well Formed Outcomes – the importance of saying it
the way you want it

"A goal is nothing more than a dream with a deadline"
Joe L. Griffith

Concept

This technique is based the NLP presupposition; Possible in the world and possible for me is only a matter of how. There are no limitations in a

> *"What is now proved, was once impossible"*
> William Blake

person's ability to learn. If another person in broadly similar circumstances to me is capable of performing a behaviour /task, then it is possible for me too, or at least improve my own performance through learning.

Benefits:

- Allows you to make S.M.A.R.T goals: Smarter.
- Broadens your horizons to view the goal from multiple perspectives.
- Compare where you are now with where you to want to be, to ensure that when you get there, you have more beneficial opportunities open to you and you can realise the positive by-products of your goal.
- To create purpose; making your outcome even more compelling, empowering yourself to move towards a solution.
- Breaks the goal down into manageable chunks; enabling you to assess your progress and establish when you have achieved your outcome.
- You get to "try your goal on" to ensure the goal is ecological and agrees with your values and beliefs.
- Ability to see a goal "As if" you already have it, allowing you to realise the additional unexpected steps you need to carry out and what other methods are available to you in order to achieve it.
- Create a "goal beyond a goal" to help prevent you from slipping back into your own ways once you have achieved it.

What is a Goal /Outcome

The Oxford English dictionary defines a Goal as a *"broad statement of what the program or person hopes to accomplish"* In NLP that simply is not good enough! A Goal is a specific outcome stated in the positive. A lot of you will have already heard of "S.M.A.R.T" outcomes, NLP takes this further reviewing the power of the words we say and whether or not the goal conflicts with our pre-existing values, beliefs and ecology.

It is important to think back to ecology when creating goals because if someone's main values are spending

> *"Don't wait for your ship to come in; swim out to it."* Anon.

time with their family then *"having a higher positioned job with a higher salary"* is not going to be an appropriate goal, if it means they are going to be working 24 hours a day 7 days a week to achieve it.

However if they stated *"It is 1st January 20XX and I have £X amount of my own money in my bank account. I spend time with my family and I am happily married to a partner I adore and who adores and supports me."* Then the goal is specific to them and their circumstances, it has a deadline and an end figure. It takes into account your conflicting value (not having as much time with family if you achieve this goal) as a positive; that your family will help and support you reach this goal.

For me John F Kennedy describes goals the best; *"We choose to go to the moon in this decade, and do the other things not because they easy, but because they are hard – because the goal will serve to organise and measure the best of our energies and skill. Because that challenge is one we are willing to accept, one we are unwilling to postpone, and one we intend to win"* In setting outcomes, we create a direction and purpose in life by which we can "programme" ourselves to consistently achieve what we want. By achieving our

> *"The purpose of life is a life of purpose"* Robert Bryne.

23

outcomes and continually reviewing and setting new outcomes, short and long term, we create the success we desire and deserve in all aspects of our life.

The difference between an outcome and a goal is that an outcome goes beyond a goal; it is the goal beyond a goal. For example competing in a 100 m local race, the goal is to come first and win, but then what? An outcome on the other hand looks at the beneficial opportunity's that come from achieving that goal, they are the stepping stones into your future, what avenues does achieving that goal open up? What will achieving that goal enable you to do? Going back to our race example, winning the race opens doors to represent your town in the county race, and then you could enter as a junior athlete and represent your country competing for gold at the Olympics. Then you can even become the fastest person to have ever ran a 100m race, the list goes on. Outcome orientation gives direction and purpose; *"Start with the end in mind"* (Steven Covey 1990) if your "end" is to just win the race then your goal has been achieved, but if it is to achieve your personal best at the Olympics then this is the goal beyond a goal. Remember the NLP presupposition; All procedures should increase choice and develop greater personal flexibility, your goal being to increase choice through having a range of techniques, facilitating flexibility.

> *"How do you eat an Elephant? One bite at a time"* Bill Hogan

Take the example of weight loss; anyone can reduce their weight if they are determined enough, but then what? The temptation to slip back into your old ways after this goal has been achieved usually results in this weight just being put back on; and there you have the classic Yo-Yo diet. But if you set the outcome "Walk 500 meters a day" that is specific to your circumstances, has a deadline and a detailed end result, then the chances of you keeping the weight off have just significantly increased.

History

In Bandler and Grinder's earliest modelling experience of Virginia Satir (Family systems therapist) and Milton Erickson (Linguistic and hypnotherapist), they discovered the basic premise of modelling excellence. One of the key differences that made Satir and Erickson excellent in their respective fields was that they were outcome oriented in their work, specifically to the outcomes that the client wanted.

Bandler and Grinder's realised that by setting a specific positive outcome, we become aware of the difference between what we have currently and what we want instead. By focusing on what we want to achieve, we pay attention to the opportunities which will assist us in achieving our desired outcome.

It is important to take into account external influences, both positive and negative as a well formed outcome is not a given. Going back to our Olympics example; you can achieve your goal (achieve your personal best at the Olympics) but not necessarily win the Gold medal as you are also competing against other athletes who are striving to achieve their personal best, which I am afraid is outside your control.

Think back to the NLP presupposition; The mind and the body affect each other. The mind and the body are one interconnected unit and so it is not possible to make changes in one without the other being affected. Likewise in the communication model, you delete, distort and generalise through your unique set of filters, the important filter here is values and beliefs. If the goal (external event) is not important to you and /or you don't believe you can do it then your most possibly right. We create our

> *To accomplish great things, we must not only act, but also dream; not only plan, but also believe.* Anatole France

own internal representation of the external event; your internal representation affects your state and therefore your behaviour which ultimately affects your results.

An example of this is Roger Bannister, Roger Bannister was determined to complete the 4 minute mile, believing it was possible against the beliefs of his doctors who said it simply was not, declaring the heart would simply combust under the strain! However in 1954 Roger had done it! With 37 more athletes breaking the 4 minute barrier over the course of the next year and this time is now the standard for all professional middle distance runners. As one of our filters; our beliefs and values have a great effect on whether or not we can achieve our goals.

It is important to remember the NLP presupposition; The person with the most choices of behaviour will have the most influence on the system (in this case, on their future). For those of you who study NLP you will recognise this as the law of requisite variety. Having multiple ways to achieve a goal will increase your chances of success because you will not give up just because you have got into difficulties. Basically the more options you have available to achieve your goal, the greater the chance of change and success.

Motivation

One other important aspect to setting goals is the motivation required to achieve them. We as humans can be categorised into being "towards" or "away from" motivated, if you think back to the communication model of NLP you will see that we delete distort and generalise information through our meta-programmes which are our personality traits (how you react to information given to you due to your personality traits i.e. how you conceptualise, perceive and comprehend information) The direction filter is one of these traits, it is the trigger that puts a person into action, whether they move towards an object /goal or away from a problem /negative consequence means that person is either towards or away from motivated.

According to Shelle Rose Charvet (1997) People with a 'towards' pattern are motivated to achieve, attain, to get, to have, whereas 'away from' people are motivated by moving away from what they don't want, to avoid, by deadlines, problems to be solved. By knowing what direction focuses you /your client, you can attain their full attention, establish a deeper rapport and avoid misunderstandings.

Carolyn Boyes (2006) expands on this, explaining that we are motivated by two types of values; a value that pull us towards something, or values that push us away from something - carrots to tempt us or sticks to punish. By being aware of this and asking yourself /the client what is important to you /them about achieving your /their goal, enables you to attain by which direction you /they are motivated. With this knowledge you can structure your language to motivate yourself /the client to focus on getting what you /they want, by either assigning tasks /setting goals or by stating what you /they would avoid if you /they do it. That is people are motivated "towards" achieving a goal or motivated "away from" what they have now.

It is also important to realise that a Goal or an outcomes can never be "to find happiness" as this is a state which can be recalled at any time from past experiences. The following chart describes the differences between Goals & Outcomes verses States further. Through a goal you can achieve a state but a state will not have enough drive to achieve a goal, as states are achievable through other multiple means.

State versus Goal

Value or State (Confidence)	Goal or Outcome (£1m, be married, weigh 12 stone)
State ambiguously	Stated specifically
Write affirmations	Write goals /outcomes
You can have it now	Time is involved
No steps	Steps are needed to get there (get final step and work backwards)
Infinite	Measurable
State for self and /or others	Stated for self only

Ok, I get outcomes, where does the "Well formed" bit come in?

This is the term used in NLP to describe a process of systematically refining goals, objectives or targets so that they fulfill the criteria. The process is similar but more thorough than that of the more widely-known process called S.M.A.R.T goals. When our wants, dreams or wishes are refined using this process they become more believable and realisable. This is why they are then described as being 'well-formed' outcomes

The term 'well-formed' has been around in NLP for over 35 years and, as with many of the rather strange NLP terms, this name can get in the way of understanding the simplicity of the model. Some people, to make things even more obtuse, even refer to it as the 'well-formedness conditions for an outcome'. Simply put, what the term really means is that the outcome has been refined or checked against eight tests and once it has 'passed' these tests it is well-designed (well-formed!) You can use this process to clarify your own wishes so that they are more realistic and action-focused - and to assist others in doing the same.

Well-formedness Conditions *(Adapted From Ian McDermott)*

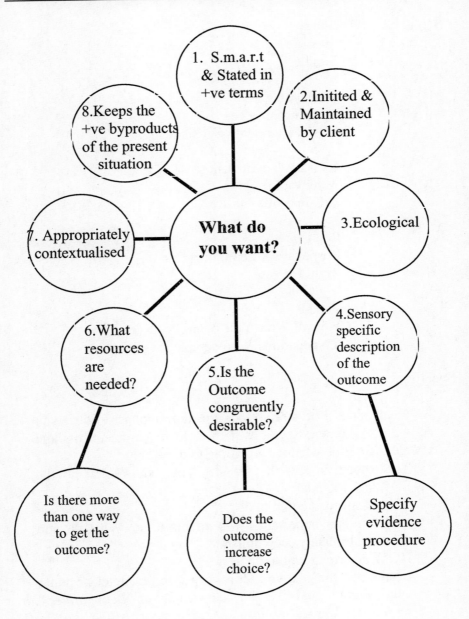

S.M.A.R.T Outcomes

S	Short Specific Simple
M	Measurable Meaningful to you More than one way to achieve it
A	As if now, in present tense Achievable All areas of your life
R	Realistic Responsible /Ecological Right for you
T	Timed Toward What You Want, Positive (no negations & no comparatives)

Specific

- Goals should be straightforward and emphasise what you want to happen. Specifics help us to focus our efforts and clearly define what we are going to do.
- The specifics are the What, Why, and How of the **S.M.A.R.T** model.
- **WHAT** are you going to do?
- **WHY** is this important to do at this time? What do you want to ultimately accomplish?
- **HOW** are you going to do it?
- Ensure that the goal you set is very specific and clear rather than setting a goal like *"To lose weight"* or *"Be healthier"*, set a specific goal *"To lose 2cm off your waistline"* or *"To walk 500 meters a day"* or *"To drink 1.5L of water a day"*.

Measurable

How will you know when the goal is accomplished? In the broadest sense, if you can't measure it, you can't manage it. The way you state your goal is a measure of the project itself. Choose a goal with measurable progress, so you can see the change occur and the progress towards achievement. What will you see, hear, feel or be doing? How will you see the success when you reach your goal? Be specific! *"I will fit into size 12 clothes before my birthday"* shows the specific target to be measured. *"I want to fit into my old clothes"* is not as measurable.

> *"I never ran 1000 miles. I could have never done that. I ran one mile 1000 times"*
> Stu Mittleman

Make sure you have established concrete criteria for measuring your progress towards the achievement of each goal you set. When you measure your progress, you stay on track, reach your target dates, and experience the exhilaration of achievement that spurs you on to the continued effort required to reach your goals.

Achievable

When you identify the goals that are most important to you, you begin to figure out ways in which you can make them come true. You develop the attitudes, abilities, skills and financial capacity to reach them and you start to notice opportunities that you had not previously seen because you are focused on your goal.

However setting goals that are too far out of your reach will probably result in poor commitment and you being half prepared to fail, even though you may start with the best of intentions, the knowledge that the goal is too much for you will result in your subconscious reminding you of this fact; preventing you from giving the goal your best effort.

So set your goal just outside your comfort zone, a goal that will take real commitment from you to achieve it. Because the sense of achievement you feel, as you progress towards fulfilling your goal, will spur you on to achieve it. For instance, losing 20lbs in one week isn't possible. But setting a goal to lose 1lb could be, once you have done that, aim to lose a further 1lb, and keep on setting these goals so that they are achievable for you. This feeling of success will help you to remain motivated.

<u>Realistic</u>

This is not a synonym for 'easy' Realistic, in this case, means 'do-able' It means that the learning curve is not a vertical slope, that the skills needed to do the work are available and that the project fits within the overall strategy and goals of the organisation. A realistic project may push the skills and knowledge of the people working on it but it shouldn't break them.

> *"Enjoyment appears at the boundary between boredom and anxiety, when the challenges are just balanced with the person's capacity to act"* Mihaly Csikszentmihalyi

Start by planning a way to get there which makes the goal realistic, the goal needs to be realistic for you and where you are at the moment. A goal of *"Never eating sweets, cakes, crisps and chocolate again"* is not exactly realistic for someone who really enjoys these foods. A more realistic goal would be to eat a piece of fruit each day instead of one sweet item. You can then choose to work towards reducing the amount of sweet products gradually as and when this feels realistic for you. Be sure to set goals that you can achieve with some effort! Too difficult and you set the stage for failure, but too low sends the message that you aren't very capable. Set the bar high enough for a satisfying achievement!

<u>Timely</u>

Set a timeframe for the goal: for next week, in three months, by fifth grade. Putting an end point on your goal gives you a clear target to work towards a dead line. If you don't set a time, the commitment is too vague. It tends not to happen because you feel you can start at any time. Without a time limit, there's no urgency. The time you set must be measurable, achievable and realistic.

<u>Examples of a **S.M.A.R.T** outcome:</u>

"It is 1st January 20XX and I own a 4 bedroom house with a ½ acre garden and a garage, within 20 minutes of my office in Wembley."

"It is 1st January 20XX and I weigh 70kg. I feel fit, strong and healthy, and have exercised for more than 1 hour at a time, more than 3 times per week for the past 6 months and enjoy it."

<u>The PACER model by Francis Wardle (2007);</u> The steps towards a well formed outcome:

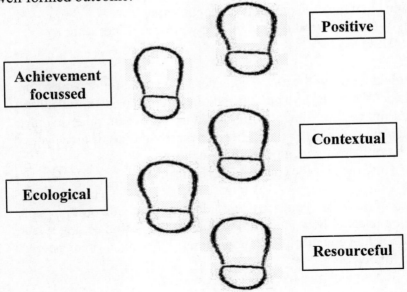

Positive. Positive means stated in terms of something you want rather than something you want to avoid. To turn a negative outcome into a positive one: ask

- What do you want?
- What will that bring you?
- What else?

Achievement focussed. It is important to think about how you will know you are succeeding and how you will know you have succeeded so that you can assess your progress. What type of feedback will give you this information? What will you hear, see and feel when you have succeeded. Make sure you know what the first steps towards your outcome will be and that they are achievable.
- How will you know when you have got it?
- How will someone else know you have got it?

Contextual. You will want to think about the contexts in which you want or don't want this outcome. There may be some situations in which the outcome is inappropriate.
- When, where and with who do you want it /not want it?
- How long for?

Ecological. You will want to consider how achieving the outcome will affect the wider system. It may have an impact on resources such as finance and time. It may have an impact on other people, on other roles you play in your life and on the choices it gives you.
- Are there any negative consequences?
- How Ok is it for you to achieve this goal?

Resourceful. Can you start and maintain the outcome? This condition is about how much direct control the person setting it has over the achievement of the outcome and how much other people will be involved.
- What resources have you got already?
- What resources do you need?

Positive By-products (From Ian McDermott)

In all behaviour there is a positive intention, otherwise you wouldn't do it. Whether you are helping yourself or others bring about change, it is important to remember that there may be positive aspects of your /their old behaviour that you /they may want to keep. Spending some time identifying what these by-products are, will enable you to make sure that you /they can keep these positive elements and so facilitate the change. This also ensures that the change is appropriate and ecological for the person /organisation, because if it loses those positive by-products it could impair the achievement of the goal.

Whether you wish to bring about individual or organisational change, the questions below will help you identify the positive by-products:

Personal	Organisational
What is this behaviour doing for me?	What functions /purpose does this behaviour or practice perform?
What are the positive by-products of my present behaviour?	What are the positive by-products of the present behaviour or practice for the individuals doing it and for the larger system?
What else happens, directly or indirectly, when I do this?	What else happens, directly or indirectly, as a result of this behaviour or practice?
What do I get out of doing this?	What do they get out of doing this?
What else do I get out of doing this?	What else do they or others get out of doing this?
What of this is worth keeping?	What of this, in their opinion, that is valuable and worth keeping?

<u>How to do it!</u> – Keys to an achievable outcome

The below exercise can be carried out by you when making goals for yourself, or with another when making goals for them;

> *Our ideals resemble the stars, which illuminate the night. No one will ever be able to touch them. But the men who, like the sailors on the ocean, take them for guides will undoubtedly reach their goal.* Carl Schurz

1. **Establish** where you /the other person is now; describe the current situation in your /their own words.

2. Get the scores on the doors, (a convincer if you will of the increased possibility of you /them achieving the goal) score, out of 10 the current possibility of them achieving this goal (1 being no possibility, 10 being "I can achieve this goal").

3. Make the outcome S.M.A.R.T and state as a positive.
   Don't use negative words such as lose, don't, unwell.
   For example: in relation to weight loss use; *"To weigh 12 stone by 1st December 20xx"*, rather than *"To lose 2 stone by 1st December 20xx"*.

4. Ensure the goal is initiated and maintained by yourself /the client; ask questions like: do you need other people to do it for you? (other people are out of you /the clients control and may adversely affect the outcome) Outcomes ideally need to be set up and carried out by yourself /the client.

5. Is the goal ecological?
- For what purpose do you want this?
- What will you gain or lose if you have it?
- What will happen if you get it?
- What won't happen if you get it?
- What will happen if you don't get it?
- What won't happen if you don't get it?
- Are there any negative consequences in achieving this goal?

6. Specific sensory based description of the outcome.
- What will you see?
- What will you hear?
- What will you feel?
    - Specify evidence procedure.
- How will you know when you have it?
- Make it compelling?
- Make it as if you have it now

7. Is the outcome congruently desirable?
- What will the outcome get for you?
- What will the outcome allow you to do?
    - Does the outcome increase choice.
- What other options are there available to you?

8. What resources are needed?
- What resources do you have now and what do you need to achieve your outcome?
- Have you ever done this before?
    - Is there more than one way to achieve the outcome?
- What other avenues are there available to you?
- Do you know anyone who has done this before who can advise you?

9. Is it appropriately Contextualised
- Where, when, how and with whom do you want it?
- What will you gain or lose if you have it?
- What will happen if you get it?
- What won't happen if you get it?

10. Keeps the positive by-products of the present situation
- Do you lose anything from achieving this outcome?

11. Read /show the client all you have written down and ask,
- "Out of 10, how possible is it to achieve this goal?"

You are looking for a 10/10, if this is not the answer, get curious and ask yourself /the client
"What would need to happen for it to be a 10/10?" and /or
"What is stopping it from being a 10/10?"

This answer may mean that the goal needs to be redefined or that a process goal needs to be established first. If this is the case then, design the goal in the same way, using steps 1-10 keeping the original goal, just checking that the timings are appropriate.

Then check again *"Out of 10, how possible is it to achieve this goal?"*

N.B this is for both goals.

Summary

A Goal is a specific target you want to achieve within a given context.

An Outcome is the future benefits of achieving the goal within the given contexts; it is the goal beyond a goal.

Goals and Outcomes are not states, they may result in a state but they are not the achievement of a state.

When it comes to well formed outcomes it is important to state it in the positive, basically: Say It the Way You Want It!

Making outcomes sensory specific asks you to see what you will see, feel what you will feel and hear what you will hear when you have this outcome in the future, making that outcome much more real, compelling and achievable.

Outcomes direct a person's thoughts and actions. Use them for your goals, dreams, and wishes - and watch what happens. The 11 well formed outcome steps distinguish between those factors which are relevant to getting what you want and those which are in the realm of history, complaint, etc.

The most important thing about goals is to set clear and concise goals that can be seen, felt and recited to ourselves regularly to keep us on track of achieving them. Where most people fail in goal setting is by not getting every aspect of the goal congruent with themselves.

One way to make goals really empowering is to adjust the submodalities of the goal making it even more achievable and desirable. So let's now make your well formed outcomes real......

Chapter 4

Submodalities – the brains language

"Surely, the brain must hold the key to human nature: understanding it will allow us to make sense of so much that puzzles us about ourselves"
Adam Zeman

Concept

This technique is based on the NLP presupposition; we are in charge of our mind and therefore our results. If we are not getting the results we want then it is up to us to change the way we are going about it so that we do get the results we want. If we do not achieve something then it is only ever our fault and our responsibility to change, in order to achieve it.

What are submodalities?

We have five basic senses through which we take in information; visual (sight), auditory (hearing), kinaesthetic, (feeling), olfactory (smell) and gustatory (taste), In NLP, these are called modalities, they are how we code, order and give meaning to our experiences, therefore having a great impact upon how we perceive what goes on around us,

Within each of these modalities, we have sub-modalities that are finer distinctions by which we give meaning to our experiences. For example, in visual terms, common distinctions include: brightness, colour contrast, size, distance, sharpness, focus, location, and so on; in auditory: volume, loud or soft, pitch, tonal range, distance, clarity, timbre, etc. Kinaesthetic: internal /external, intensity, still or moving, heavy or light (feeling), hot or cold, high pressure /low pressure etc.

> *"A man cannot directly choose his circumstances, but he can choose his thoughts, and so indirectly, yet surely, shape his circumstances."*
> James Allen

How would you remember what someone was wearing or how they looked the last time you saw them? How can you compare what someone looked liked 6 weeks ago to 6 months ago? You code the two different memories in different submodalities. We create meaning by using different submodalities that code our experience, if we didn't, how would we be able to differentiate between 6 weeks, 6 months or 6 years ago?

The technique of changing submodalities is an extremely useful and powerful technique that can change the meaning of an experience; to be less negative, more positive and more empowering. By changing how people represent their own internal representations of themselves, whether past or future orientated, we can help them become more resourceful. For example, changing an internal picture of a goal to be; more colourful, brighter, clearer, bigger and closer (if that is what works for you) you will make it more appealing, empowering and increase your motivation to achieve it.

Examples of Visual, Auditory, Kinaesthetic submodalities;

Visual Submodalities	Auditory Submodalities	Kinaesthetic Submodalities
Size of Picture	Volume	Location
Big /Med /Small	High or Low(Pitch)	Size
Near or Far	Tempo: Fast or Slow	Shape
Location	Direction of sounds	Colour
Black & White or Colour	Internal or External Direction of Sounds	Intensity High or Low
Bright or Dim	Sharp or Soft	Texture: Rough or Smooth
Associated or Dissociated	Timbre: Clear or Raspy	Still or Moving
Number of Pictures	Cadence or Rhythm	Hot or Cold
Focused or Defocused	Pauses	Fast or Slow
Focus: Changing or Steady	Duration of Sounds	Heavy or Light
	Uniqueness of sound	Duration: Short or Long
	Location of Sounds	

How are they useful? Well let's take the following phrase:

"X (the goal) is out of my reach"

How many times have you heard that being said?

Without eliciting the submodalities, the phrase suggests that the goal is out in front of them (Location) and far away (near or far), how would they feel if this goal was directly in front of them (near) and touchable? Altering the location, distance and size changes the viewpoint of whether a goal can or cannot be achieved.

How about that "voice inside (internal) your head?" The one that criticises chastises and says you can't achieve that goal?

> "*That voice inside your head is not the voice of God. It just sounds like it thinks it is*" Cheri Huber

What would be the impact if you changed that voice to sound like Mickey Mouse (Pitch) or if you turned the volume down (Volume) or if you made it into a seductive voice (Tempo: slow)

Finally a Kinaesthetic example would be a phrase like;

"X (the goal) will put me under too much pressure"

This suggests that the feeling of pressure is high, heavy, and above them from the phrase. We could assume this feeling is an "angry" colour such as a shade of red, so what would happen if we turned the colour to be blue? (Colour) or if we associated this "pressure" with a comical shape (shape) or as heavy as a feather (heavy or light). If this pressure was no longer above them (Location) but was beneath them, or to the left, to the right or in front of them, so that they can acknowledge and act upon it, what would be the impact then?

Which leads us into ecology, pressure is needed in some situations, for example if your goal is to do well in your GCSE exams. Pressure makes you aware of the importance of the situation, and so taking away the pressure is not always ecological. Submodalities can be used to take away the stress, numbness or the overwhelming feeling pressure may bring to allow you to realise the pressures significance, then remove these restricting feelings and get on with the task in hand.

I want you to remember a goal you have achieved, it does not matter how big or small it was, just the fact you have achieved it. Maybe it relates to a personal goal, a goal at work or simply operating your new washing machine. An achievement that you have made, that you had not done before.

Now close your eyes and go back to that time when you realised you had done it, picture that scene in your mind, what do you see? Is it a black and white, or colour? Or is it a moving film or a still picture? Is it bright or dim? Are you looking through your own eyes or do you see yourself in the picture? Note down the details and how you perceive the scene.

The answers to those questions are your submodalities for that experience, in other words, how you see the scene now is how you represent that experience to yourself. Seeing the experience is the modality, the way you see it is the submodality; the experience for you.

Now go through the same process with a goal you have not achieved. Maybe you felt frustrated, disappointed, even angry with yourself, and answer the same questions about the scene; what do you see? Is it a still photo? Is it like a movie scene from a film? Is it in black and white or colour? Is it bright or dim? Are you looking at yourself in the scene or looking through your own eyes? Again note down the details, and compare these answers to the answers of your "achieved goal" experience above. You will find that there are major differences between the two, which will be different for each and every one of us and represent how we code, order and give meaning to an event.

By changing these representations, you will change the meaning of that event to yourself. Like a film director, if you change your unachieved goal scene to be more like your achieved goal scene, you will change your experience. It is important to remember that submodalities are not the solution to the problem; they simply empower us by taking the emotional charge out of a situation, enabling us to be in a more resourceful state to work out the solution.

History

Unlike a lot of the other techniques you will learn in NLP that have been "discovered" or modelled, having existed previously as part of some long lost culture or one of the modern discoveries made by such pre-NLP schools as Chomsky's transformational grammar, Ericksonian Hypnosis or Fritz Pearls' methodology of Gestalt Therapy, nothing similar to submodalities has ever existed in the past. There has been reference to them in the way that people are able to code, order and give meaning to experience and describe their feelings through pictures of memories but never in the form of the submodalities that we know today.

Submodalities was developed by Richard Bandler one of the co-founders of NLP through his study into Pragmagraphics which is an area of NLP established by Todd Epstein and Richard Bandler in 1980. This has been further developed by Epstein with Robert Dilts over the following decade. Submodalities relate back to the NLP definition of a wanton curiosity, as it was Richard Bandler's curiosity of holography to the human brain that brought about the work of submodalities.

Richard Bandler and Todd Epstein's holography, is the study of work done by the Stanford neurophysiologist Karl Pribram that was carried out in the 1960's, where he hypothesized that memories are encoded not in neurons, or small groupings of neurons, but in patterns of nerve impulses that crisscross the entire brain in the same way that patterns of laser light interference crisscross the entire area of a piece of film containing a holographic image. In other words, Pribram believes the brain is itself a hologram. He backed up this theory with the thoughts that explains how the human brain can store so many memories in so little space (It has been estimated that the human brain has the capacity to memorize something on the order of 10 billion bits of information during the average human lifetime) which is understandable if the brain functions according to holographic principles.

If a friend asks you to tell him what comes to mind when he says the word "zebra", you do not have to clumsily sort back through some gigantic and cerebral alphabetic file to arrive at an answer. Instead, associations like "striped", "horselike", and "animal native to Africa" all pop into your head instantly. Indeed, one of the most amazing things about the human thinking process is that every piece of information seems instantly cross-correlated with every other piece of information, another feature intrinsic to the hologram. Because every portion of a hologram is infinitely interconnected with every other portion, it is perhaps nature's supreme example of a cross-correlated system.

Much like a hologram Epstein hypothesized a particular submodality picture (the clarity of an internal image for example) could function like the reference beam used to make a hologram. Altering this submodality like adjusting the angle or wavelength of the reference beam would change the resulting interference pattern bringing out different dimensions and facets of the experiences of which it was linked, perhaps shifting it to something else altogether.

Going back to the "What are submodalities" section above, I have tried to give vague examples and descriptions whilst explaining the practical usage of submodalities because submodalities are different for every person. If I may highlight my "I feel under so much pressure" example, when I am under pressure I visualise a purple pulsing anvil weight as big as the ceiling as the room I am in hanging over me, whereas you could image pressure as a big spiky red cloud floating around your head. Submodalities are different from person to person, they are how a person perceives /visualises /hears and feels about their problem.

Eliciting submodalities help us to avoid guessing, making generalisations and mind reading. Whereas changing submodalities is not the solution to the problem, they do empower us by taking the emotional charge out of a situation, enabling us to be in a more resourceful state to work out the solution.

Think back to the NLP presupposition; People have all the resources they need to make the changes they want. People themselves are not un-resourceful, they are simply experiencing un-resourceful states, which when changed allows them to access all the resources within them to accomplish whatever they choose.

Also think back to the communication model of NLP and subjective experience, the internal representation is what we store as our memory of the external event. Submodalities are how we code this internal representation which effects are state, physiology and behaviour. By changing the submodalities of an experience you can impact upon how that experience affects you today, changing the internal representation to be more positive will affect your state and physiology which is reflected in your behaviour and therefore your results, enabling you to be more motivated and work from a more resourceful state.

How it works

Pull up your goal and notice all the modalities and submodalities; are they as congruent as the submodalities associated with a goal you have already achieved? Odds are they are qualitatively different indicating what you have pulled up is a wish and not yet a certainty. Check out your goal and the picture, sounds and feelings associated with it. Is it congruent with your purpose? Do you feel excited by it? Ask yourself if any other parts of you would rather you didn't reach that goal? When you have congruence with all parts of that future goal, when you are positive that it is something you want to achieve, then pull up the sounds, picture, and feelings. Adjust all the submodalities one by one until they are identical to the ones you had associated with your past achieved goal.

47

When you have it totally tweaked, so that it is identical in all aspects, notice how you feel about it. If you still feel good and there are no parts objecting to the goal then there is now a certainty about your goal and a power associated to it which it previously lacked. A point to make here is that the past achieved goal has to be a goal that you not only achieved, but enjoyed, were excited by, happy about or looked forward to completing. If you do this properly you will find yourself drawn towards things (that you would not have noticed before) that will drive you towards achieving your goal. Another benefit will be the acquired ability to accept or reject things which would either help or hinder your path towards the goal. Soon you will find that achieving your goal is no longer a struggle, but an automated response.

In NLP there are two main types of Submodalities that bring about this change of internal representation and therefore changes in a person's state, physiology and behaviour, these are;

Critical Submodalities and Driver Submodalities

Critical Submodalities make the difference in the meaning of an experience, some of the submodalities are more critical than others. For the majority of people, location, size and whether the picture is associated (looking through your own eyes) or dissociated (looking at yourself in the picture) are the most critical. If the picture had a negative emotion attached to it and was located in front of you, just by moving it down to the bottom left (for example, depending on the person!) will take the emotional charge from it.

A Driver submodality is a submodality so important that it affects all the other submodalities when you change it. If location was the driver submodality, then you would find that the colour, size, brightness and distance (for example, again dependant on the person) will have changed as soon as you move it down to the bottom left.

The two main ways in which you can use submodalities in order to be in charge of your results are;

1) Alter the submodalities of an internal representation
2) Mapping across

Firstly, Alter the submodalities of an internal representation.

Do this exercise with a friend /family member that you feel comfortable with and trust. The other person is carrying out the exercise on you.

> "I am always doing things I can't do – that's how I get to do them"
> Pablo Picasso

Get your friend to follow the script below, with your friend asking you to identify a picture of a 'Goal' you want to make more compelling and attractive. Elicit each of the submodalities, using the following submodality checklist, making changes to each submodality one by one, with your friend asking whether the change makes it better, worse, or no difference.

If worse or no difference, your friend needs to tell you to change it back, keep the changes that make it better and if you notice that a certain change makes it a lot better than change that submodality further. For example if "making it bigger" creates a change for the better then your friend tells you to carry on making it even bigger and bigger until it feels right for you.

Altering Submodalities Script - The Process

Conducted by your friend

1) Ask "*Can you think of the goal (well Formed Outcome) that you want to make more compelling?*"

2) Here is where the ecology comes in, ask:
   "*Are there any negative consequences of making this change?*"
   "*What would happen if you made it more compelling?*"

49

"What would happen if you left it as it was?"
"What wouldn't happen if you made it more compelling?"
"What wouldn't happen if you didn't make it more compelling?"

3) Ask again: *"Think of the goal and get a picture"*

4) Elicit the submodalities using the submodality checklist (on the subsequent page). Go through the checklist asking each point one after another; e.g. *"Is it black and white, or colour?""Is it near or far away?" "Where is it located?"* and so on.

5) Once you have elicited all the submodalities say *"Thank you. Now I you to want you to bring back the picture and....."* making changes to each submodality one by one, asking whether the change makes it better, worse or no difference. For example if the picture was in black and white say *"Make it colour....does that make it better, worse or no difference?"*

6) Keep the changes that make it better, change back the changes that make it worse or no difference.

7) Lock in the changes. *Say "lock in all the changes that made it better".*

8) Test: Ask how they feel in reference to their original goal. *"How do you feel about your goal now?"*

9) Future pace Say *"Go out into the future to when you will start implementing what you need to do in order to achieve your goal"* and ask *"How do you feel now?" "What will you do differently?"* (This is done as a convincer so you both know there has been progress).

N.B Friend identifies the driver; the submodality that made the difference. They ask *"Which question /submodality difference made the biggest difference?"* For you to know this is very empowering, as you will be able to apply this method to other things for yourself. (We are in charge of our mind then we are in charge of our results).

Submodalities Checklist

VISUAL				
Near or Far				Can you make a picture ?
Bright or Dim				
Location				
Size of Picture				
Associated or Dissociated				
Focused or Defocused				
Focus-Changing or Steady				
Framed or Panoramic				
Movie or Still				
Moving Speed				
Amount of Contrast				
3D or Flat				
Angle Viewed From				
# of Picture				
AUDITORY	******	******	*******	
Location				Are there any Sounds that are Important ?
Direction				
Internal or External				
Loud or Soft				
Fast or Slow				
High or Low(Pitch)				
Timbre-Clear or Raspy				
Pauses				
Cadence or Rhythm				
Duration				
Uniqueness of sound				

51

KINESTHETIC	*******	******	*******
Location			
Size			
Shape			
Colour			
Intensity			
Steady			
Still or Moving			
Fast or Slow			
Duration-Short or Long			
Humidity-Dry or Wet			
Vibration			
Hot or Cold			
Pressure-High or Low			
Texture-Rough or Smooth			
Heavy or Light			
Internal or External			

Are there any Feelings that are important?

The Second way in which you can use submodalities is by a process called; Mapping across.

Mapping across is a two step process of carrying out "Contrastive analysis" and then a procedure called "Mapping across". Where you elicit the submodalities of two internal representations; the goal you want to achieve and a really successful goal you have achieved and then change the submodalities of the goal you want to achieve to be the same as the submodalities of the really successful goal you have achieved, just as we have spoken about previously.

1. Contrastive Analysis

Contrastive analysis is the elicitation of the two goals separately and then comparing and contrasting the submodalities of the two different goals /internal representations against each other. Finding the critical submodality, this if you remember, is the submodality that defines the desired state to the undesired state.

2. Mapping Across

Mapping across is changing the undesired state submodalities to be the same as the desired state ones. Mapping across is discovering the drivers, drivers are the submodalities that make the other submodalities change, and then changing the submodalities of the undesired state into that of the desired state.

Essentially, mapping across allows us to change, where appropriate, a goal you want to be compelling, into a very compelling achievable goal. This is done by changing the submodalities of the desired goal picture into the submodalities of the successfully completed goal picture. When the mapping across is completed, whenever you think of your desired goal you will find that you have a very appealing picture in your mind.

Submodalities Mapping Across Script

Conducted by your friend

1. Ask *"Can you think of goal which you want to achieve, a well formed goal?"*

2. Make sure you have a well formed goal before you start, that is a S.M.A.R.T goal.

3. Here is where the ecology comes in, ask:

"Are there are any negative consequences of making this change?"
"What would happen if you made it more compelling?"
"What would happen if you left it as it was?"
"What wouldn't happen if you made it more compelling?"
"What wouldn't happen if you didn't make it more compelling?"

4. *"Think of a goal that you have successfully achieved"*. Remember the closer the goals are to each other the better.

5. Elicit the submodalities of the desired well formed goal, using the submodality elicitation script.

6. Elicit the submodalities of a goal that you have achieved, are committed to achieving or are in the process of achieving.

7. Do the contrastive analysis and look for the driver, i.e. the differences from one to the other remembering the critical submodalities and the drivers.

8. Do the mapping across, saying *"**Make** the submodalities of the desired well formed goal into the already achieved successful /committed goal"*.

9. Say *"Lock in the changes"*. You could say like a key in a lock.

10. Test: Ask how they feel in reference to their original goal. *"How do you feel about your goal now?"*

11. Future pace Say *"Go out into the future to when you will start implementing what you need to do in order to achieve your goal"* and ask *"How do you feel now?" "What will you do differently?"* (This is done as a convincer so you both know there has been progress).

N.B Remember to identify the driver, the submodality that made the difference, Friend asks *"Which question /submodality difference made the biggest difference?"* For you to know this is very empowering as you will be able to apply this method to other things for yourself. (Remember the NLP presupposition: we are in charge of our mind then we are in charge of our results).

Below is an example of when I changed a client's Internal Representation of her desired goal: *"I will have lost 2 inches off my waist by the 1ˢᵗ May 2009 by going to the gym 3 times a week and eating a well balanced diet, I feel confident and happy about myself"* into a goal she had achieved: *"I will drink 1L of water a day and feel healthier for it"* (a goal she does on a daily basis which had now become a habit, and she could list the health benefits it gives her) Now this lady is comfortably in size 12 clothes, which is the 2 inch loss from her waist, and feels and looks great.

VISUAL	Desired Goal	Drink 1L Water	New Picture of desired Goal
Black & white or colour	BW	C	* C
Near or Far	F	N	* N
Bright or Dim	D	B	* B
Location	Side upper	Front mid	* Front mid
Size of Picture Big /Med /Small	S	M	* M
Associated or dissociated	A	A	
Focused or Defocused	F	F	
Focus-changing /steady	C	S	* S
Framed or Panoramic	F	P	* P
Movie or Still	M	M	

Moving-Fast or Slow	S	S	
Amount of Contrast	A Little	Lots	* Lots
3D or Flat	3D	3D	
Angle Viewed From	Straight	Straight	
# of Picture	1	1	

AUDITORY	**********	*********	**********
Location	Left Side	Right Side	* Right Side
Direction	Towards Ear	Circular	* Circular
Internal or External	E	E	
Loud or Soft	S	L	* L
Fast or Slow	F	F	
High or Low(Pitch)	H	H	
Timbre-Clear or Raspy	R	C	* C
Pauses	No	No	
Cadence or Rhythm	No	No	
Duration	Long Time	Long Time	
Uniqueness of sound	No	No	

KINESTHETIC	**********	*********	**********
Location	Chest	All Over	* All Over
Size	B	Very B	* Very B
Shape	Square	Round	* Round
Colour	Blue	Green	* Green
Intensity High or Low	H	H	
Steady	No	Yes	* Yes
Still or Moving	S	M	* M
Fast or Slow	-	F	* F
Duration-Short or Long	S	S	
Humidity-Dry or Wet	D	D	
Vibration Yes or No	Y	Y	
Hot or Cold	C	Warm	* Warm
Pressure-High or Low	Yes-High	N	* N
Texture-rough or smooth	R	S	* S
Heavy or Light	H	H	
Internal or External	I	I	

Tips for making these submodalities techniques really successful:

Your friend needs to ensure that they;

1) Do the process quickly; as the unconscious mind processes quickly
2) Make sure that their attention is always on you, and not just the checklist.
3) Ask *"Do you have a picture?"* rather than *"Can you make a picture?"* if they say *"Can you?"* then you will most probably answer yes, but not necessarily have the true picture in your mind.
4) Use shorthand rather than writing full words.
5) Check ecology.

Goal Setting Strategy

Setting a strategy for goals is where a lot of people let themselves down, by not having a clear strategy! They know what they want but not always how to get there. Often goals need to be formed in stages: there might need to be several process goals like stepping stones to reach to the desired goal. They might also need to plan procedural goals, procedures that need to be in place in order for the goal to be achieved. These will be highlighted in the well formed outcome questions, all of which will need documenting and dating in the well formed outcome way.

Principles of Mapping Across

(Client = person technique is performed upon)

Identify the critical submodalities, as these are the submodalities that make the difference in the meaning of an experience.

Take charge. Tell the other person (who you are doing the exercise on) to **make** it colour, **make** it bright, **move** it to the left. If you say *"Can you?"* or *"Could you?"* the client can either say yes or no or worse; say yes, but then move it back to its original place, making the exercise ineffective and pointless as you have not given them direct instructions.

Ensure the client wants the change. If you get anything less than a congruent yes when asking if the client wants to solve their problem, or do the procedure, then get really curious into why they want to keep their problem. Get the scores on the doors as to where they are now and where they want to get to. The client needs to be 100% committed to wanting the change. If the client says they are only 80% committed, get curious.

Same context - Ensure what you are changing is in the same context; changing submodalities associated with writing notes into swimming is not likely to work.

Ecology - If the change doesn't sit right with you then I would urge you not to do it. You need to check that there are no negative consequences for the client, the client's friends, family, neighbours and society, in fact the planet in general. Also check yourself, if there is any incongruence with you, as this will mirror back to the client and make the technique potentially unsuccessful. Remember congruence, if you don't get a congruent answer then don't do it and investigate why.

One note here is that with food: do not change a food they dislike into a food they like. There is usually a very good reason why a

58

person doesn't like a food, for example you are allergic. There is also **a lot** of psychology attached to food and I am sure the Dieticians and the Doctors reading this will have seen patients who have negative memories around certain foods. For example being force fed, abused or bullied.

<u>Summary</u>

Submodalities are how we code, order and give meaning to our experiences (through are five basic senses of visual, auditory, kinaesthetic, olfactory and gustatory) if we have coded it one way then just as easily (by changing the submodalities) we can code it another; changing its order and meaning during the process.

Submodalities are fantastic in goal setting as they bring the goal alive, they make it bigger, brighter and closer to you (if that is what works for you) making it even more compelling and achievable.

Submodalities is a simple technique that can completely transform the difficulty in which completing the goal is being viewed from, as long as you act ecologically and ensure it is congruent to your values and believes.

Chapter 5: Exercises!

Exercise 1 – define you!

The most important things in the world to me are:
1.
2.
3.
4.
5.

If I could be /do anything in the world I would:

_____

_____

I Know I am succeeding when:

_____

_____

My skills, qualities, gifts, talents:

_____

_____

Exercise 2 – Write a S.M.A.R.T goal

As outlined in the exercise above, for example: *"It is 1 January 20XX and I own a 4 bedroom house with a ½ acre garden and a garage, within 20 minutes of my office in Wembley."*

Exercise 3 – Write a Well formed outcome

Rewrite your goal above following the keys to an achievable outcome on page 36, this can either be done individually or in pairs of 2, where Person A is the 'client' and Person B is the NLPer carrying out the exercise.

Exercise 4

All the below exercises involve two people – Person A is the 'client', Person B is the NLPer carrying out the exercise.

1. Persons B elicits Person A's submodalities of the well formed outcome using the eliciting submodalities script on Page 49.
2. Swap over so that Person A has the opportunity to elicit submodalities.

Exercise 5

1. Now these submodalities have been elicited, Person B thanks Person A and then starts to ask them to bring back the picture and make changes to each submodality one by one, asking whether the change makes it better, worse or no difference. For example if the picture was in black and white, tell the client to *"Make it colour... does that make it better, worse or no difference?"*

2. Person B tells Person A to keep the changes that make it better, telling Person A to change back the changes that made it worse or had no effect.

3. Person B tells Person A to lock in all the changes that made it better.

4. Test: Person B asks Person A how they feel in reference to their original goal. *"How do you feel about your goal now?"*

5. Future pace: Person B asks Person A *to "Go out into the future to when you will start implementing what you need to do in order to achieve your goal"* and ask *"How do you feel now?" "What will you do differently?"* (This is done as a convincer so you both know there has been progress).

6. After there has been a successful change, swap places so that Person A has the opportunity to elicit submodalities.

Exercise 6

1. Person B follows the mapping across submodalities script from page 53.

2. Person B tells Person A to *"Think of a goal which you want to achieve, a well formed goal?"*

3. Person A needs to make sure that they have a well formed goal before they start, that is a S.M.A.R.T goal.

4. Here is where the ecology comes in, Person B asks:

   "Are there any negative consequences of making this change?"
   "What would happen if you made it more compelling?"
   "What would happen if you left it as it was?"
   "What wouldn't happen if you made it more compelling?"
   "What wouldn't happen if you didn't make it more compelling?"

5. Person B says *"Think of a goal that you have successfully achieved"*. Remember the closer the goals are to each other the better.

6. Person B elicits the submodalities of the desired well formed goal, using the submodality elicitation script on page 49.

7. Person B then elicits the submodalities of a goal that Person A has achieved, is committed to achieving or is in the process of achieving.

8. Person B then performs the contrastive analysis, and looks for the driver, i.e. the differences between the desired goal and the achieved goal, remembering the critical submodalities and the drivers.

9. Person B then performs the mapping across, **telling** Person A to "*Make the submodalities of the desired well formed goal into the already achieved /successful /committed goal*".

10. Person B tells Person A to "*Lock in the changes*".

11. Test: Person B asks Person A how they feel in reference to their original goal. "*How do you feel about your goal now?*"

12. Future pace: Person B asks Person A to "*Go out into the future to when you will start implementing what you need to do in order to achieve your goal*" and ask "*How do you feel now?*" "*What will you do differently?*" (This is done as a convincer so you both know there has been progress).

13. After there has been a successful change, swap places so that Person A has the opportunity to elicit submodalities and carry out the mapping across script.

Chapter 6: Conclusion

In a nutshell, we have five basic senses: visual, auditory, kinaesthetic, olfactory and gustatory, or what you and I call sight, sound, touch, smell and taste. These are the modalities, within each of these we have sub-modalities which are the finer distinctions by which we give meaning to our experiences. So the submodalities are really how you perceive your experiences, they are adjectives or feelings that come up within you, that make up your experience.

By changing the submodalities associated with a goal (Well formed outcome), we can make it more appealing and empowering to motivate yourself to achieve it.

A New Year gives us the opportunity to let go off the negative emotions of the past year and look to the future. We can all keep New Year resolutions by creating well formed outcomes and then using submodalities to make them more realistic and desirable. Before you go I would like to amalgamate the teachings off this book into the useful hints below:

Hints for achieving New Year's Resolutions

Don't spread yourself to thin

Make Only One Resolution – Most people make the mistake of trying to achieve too much. The chances of success are greater when people channel their energy into changing just one aspect of their behaviour.

Plan ahead

Don't wait until New Year's Eve to think about your resolution. Last minute decisions tend to be based on what is on your mind at that time. Instead, take some time out a few days before and reflect upon what you really want to achieve.

Avoid making past resolutions

Making a past resolution brings about memory's of frustration and disappointment. Choose something new, or approach an old problem in a new way. For example, instead of trying to lose 2 stone in weight, try exercising more.

Be specific

Think through exactly what you are going to do, where you are going to do it, and at what time. Vague plans fail. For example, instead of saying that you will go running two days of the

> *"Motivation is what gets you started. Habit is what keeps you going"* Jim Ryun

week, tell yourself that you will run on Tuesdays and Thursdays at 6pm. These become dates in your dairy, instead of tasks that can be pushed back to the end of the week, which inevitably means something crops up preventing you from doing it or you are too tired from exercising the day before to exercise today.

Make it personal

Don't run with the crowd and go with the usual resolutions. Instead think about what you really want out of life, so think about finishing that novel, or learning to play an instrument, rather than just losing weight and getting to the gym.

Set Well Formed outcomes

Focus on creating goals that are Specific, Measurable, Achievable, Realistic and Time based (S.M.A.R.T). For example, instead of thinking 'I want to find a new job', focus on creating bite-sized, measurable goals for each week, such as investigating the market of your desired role, investigate the company you wish to work for in that desired market, rewriting your CV... Map out the step-by-step mini-goals that will slowly but surely take you to where you want to be, make a note of them in a diary, and stick to the plan.

Get Motivated!

Focus on how much better life will be for you, and those around you, when you achieve your resolution. For example, if you want to quit smoking, make a list of the benefits of giving up, and place it somewhere prominent in your house. If you want to motivate yourself to go to the gym, find a photograph of a fitness model that appeals to you, and put it in a place that ensures you will see it each day.

Go public

Many people keep their New Year's Resolution to themselves. Unfortunately, this makes it all too easy to simply forget about them. Instead, go public. For example, write down your resolution on a large sheet of paper, sign it, and place it

> *"If all you did was tell a lamppost your goals for each day, they would still be far more likely to happen"*
> Michael Neill

somewhere prominent in your house. Tell your friends, family and colleagues about your resolution, and ask them to provide you with helpful nudges to assist you in achieving your goal. Either way, do not keep your resolution to yourself.

Be persistent

New habits take time to learn, and once in a while you will slip up and revert to the old you. People on diets might suddenly give in to temptation, or those trying to exercise more might not find the time to go to the gym for a week. Remember that everyone messes up from time to time. Don't blame yourself if you falter, or allow the experience to make you give up.

A goal should lead to a better life for you, that is, a goal is easy to achieve as your new life schedules it in, it becomes part of who you are and

> *"We first make our habits, then our habits make us"* John Dryden

what you enjoy thus becoming easier the more you perform and integrate it into your life, instead of giving up half way through.

References

- Andreas, S., Andreas, C. (1987) *Change Your Mind and Keep The Change*. Utah, Real People Press
- Bandler, R. (1985) *Using Your Brain for A Change*. Real People Press
- Bandler, R., Macdonald, W. (1989) *An Insiders Guide to Submodalities*. Utah, Real People Press
- www.businessballs.com/sevenhabitsstevencovey.htm
- Csikszentmihalyi, M. (1990). *Flow: The Psychology of Optimal Experience*. New York: Harper and Row
- Dilts, R. B. and DeLozier, J. (2000*) Encyclopaedia of Systemic NLP and NLP New Coding*, Scotts Valley, CA: NLP University Press. Available online at NLPuniversitypress.com
- http://twm.co.nz/hologram.html
- www.nlpu.com/Articles/artic25.htm
- Charvet, S.R. (1997) *Words That Change Minds*, Dubuque, IA: Kendall Hunt
- Boyes, C. (2006) *Need to Know? NLP Achieve Success with Positive Thinking*, London: Harper Collins.
- Wake, Lisa. Neurolinguistic Psychotherapy Routledge publishing 2008
- O'Connor, Joseph; McDermott, Ian. *Way of NLP*. Thorsons, Hammersmith, London, England, 2001.

Glossary

Association	You are inside an experience, seeing through your own eyes, fully in your senses. Experiencing something as if you are actually there.
Auditory	The representation system pertaining to hearing, including our own internal dialogue and external sounds.
Behaviour	Human activity, both physical and mental that we engage in, including thought processes.
Beliefs	The generalisations that we make about ourselves, others and the world. What we take as true.
Communication	The process of conveying information, ideas or intention, by language, signs, symbols and behaviour.
Congruence	Alignment of identity, beliefs and values, capabilities and behaviour.
Context	The particular setting or situation in which the content occurs.
Critical Submodalities	Critical submodalities are the difference that makes the difference. Discovered through the process of contrastive analysis, critical submodalities are the difference between two different internal representations. When submodalities are compared through contrastive analysis, critical submodalities are the submodalities that are different.
Deletion	Deletion occurs when we exclude part of an experience from thought or speech. One of three major processes on which the meta model is based.

Digital	Digital is a submodality that has to be one thing or another, e.g. black or white, on or off, associated or dissociated. Language is digital communication
Dissociated	Being outside an experience, seeing it as an observer rather than as a participant. As if seeing yourself in a film.
Distortion	Changing the meaning of someone else's experience, according to your map of reality. One of three major processes (including deletion and generalisation) on which the meta model is based.
Drivers	The submodality that makes the most difference in our meaning of an experience. It is so important that it carries all the other submodality differences, the critical submodalities when we change it.
Ecology	The study of the consequences or results or impact of any change that occurs on the wider system.
Ecology check	Checking the consequences of any change to ensure that it is something that is desirable for all concerned. A check on the total system implications of any course of action.
Evidence Procedure	The sensory information that will let you know that you have achieved your outcome.
Future Pace	Mentally rehearsing a future result by projecting a situation into the future so that the desired outcome automatically occurs.

Generalisation	The process by which one specific experience comes to represent a whole class of experiences. One of three major processes on which the meta model is based.
Gestalt	A collection of memories around a certain topic.
Gustatory (G)	The representational system dealing with taste.
Intention	The purpose of a behaviour or its desired outcome.
Internal Representations	The arrangement of information we create and store in our minds in the form of pictures, sounds, feelings, tastes, smells and self talk.
Kinaesthetic	The feeling sense, tactile sensations and internal feelings such as remembered sensations, emotions, and the sense of balance.
Law of Requisite Variety	In a given physical system, that part of the system with the greatest flexibility of behaviour will control the system.
Map of Reality	Each person's unique representation of the world built from his or her individual perceptions and experiences. Also referred to as 'Model of the World'.
Modality	Any one of five senses: Visual, Auditory, Kinaesthetic. Olfactory, Gustatory.
Model of the World	A person's values, beliefs and attitudes as well as their internal representations, states and physiology, that all relates to and create their belief system of how the world operates.

Neuro Linguistic Programming	NLP is the study of excellence and how the language of the mind produces our behaviour – a model of how individuals structure their experience, and the study of the structure of subjective experience.
Olfactory	The sense of smell.
Outcome	A specific sensory based desired goal, with evidence procedure.
Positive Intention	The positive purpose underlying any action or belief. The real desire that is driving the particular behaviour. NLP presupposes that every behaviour has a positive intention, even though the behaviour may seem to be self defeating.
Presuppositions of NLP	Assumptions or convenient beliefs, which are not necessarily "true", but which if accepted and believed will change our thinking and improve our results.
Rapport	A relationship of trust and responsiveness with self or others.
Representational Systems	The different channels whereby we re-present information on the inside, using our senses; visual (sight), auditory (hearing), kinaesthetic (feelings), olfactory (smell), gustatory (taste).
Resources	Anything that can help one achieve an outcome, e.g. physiology, states, thoughts, beliefs, strategies, experiences, people, events, places, possessions, procedures, techniques, stories etc.
Resourceful State	This refers to any state where a person has positive helpful emotions and

	strategies available to him or her, and is operating from them behaviourally. Obviously the state implies a successful outcome.
Secondary Gain	The reason /reward the person has or receives for not changing from a presenting problem.
Sensory Based Description	The use of words to describe, but not diagnose, an observation or experience directly verified by the senses, e.g. his jaw is clenched tightly provides a sensory based description.
State	The sum of our thoughts, feelings, emotions, physical and mental energy. In NLP, our internal representations, plus our state and our physiology results in our behaviour.
Strategy	A sequence of behaviour patterns intended to produce a specific outcome; the way we organise our ideas and behaviour in order to perform a specific task.
Submodalities	The components that make up each modality or representational system, enabling our brains to sort and code our experience.
Unconscious Mind	The part of your mind that you are not consciously aware of.
Visual	The representational system dealing with the sense of sight.
Well formedness conditions	The well formedness conditions allow us to specify outcomes that are more achievable, because the language conforms to certain rules.

Index

Also From MX Publishing

Psychobabble

A Straight forward plain English guide
to the benefits of NLP

More NLP books at www.mxpublishing.co.uk